DEEP THOUGHTS

FROM THE SHALLOW POOL

AUTHORS
Kevin Mitchell
Keith Shular

LAYOUT & DESIGN
Keith Shular

EDITOR
Simone Maroney

Blank Page Intentionally

Published by Hemingway Publishers

Cover design by Keith Shular

ISBN: Printed in the United States

KEVIN MITCHELL

I would like to dedicate my contributions to this book to my father, Anthony Edward Mitchell.

My father passed away on October 3, 2022.

He conquered his biggest demons before he passed, and I have always respected him for that. He was living proof that with love, hard work and a strong mindset, people can change.

If I can be half the man he was when he passed, mine will be a life worth living.

KEITH SHULAR

I dedicate this book to my friends and family who have stood by me and continue to provide cover fire while my mind wages war with my body and spirit.

INTRODUCTION

Do you ever feel like technology consumes you? Like powerful computer algorithms used by websites and apps for news, social media feeds, and streaming media spoon-feed you digital content to bend you to their whims?

We think it's time to step away from our robot overlords, spend some time with ourselves, and shine a light on our society's deteriorating mental health.

We've curated a collection of bite-sized, but meaningful, poems and quotes from some of history's greatest philosophers and poets. We've grouped these passages, along with selected artwork, into themes that weave together the very fabric of humanity: self-reflection, loss and grief, love and relationships, inspiration, and hope.

We hope this book will provide the spark needed by people of all ages to reignite their love for poetry and the written word. We intend for the passages in these pages to encourage people to talk with each other about their mental health, lift each other up, and share insights into how to better cope with life's challenges. Our ultimate goal is to provide a resource that people can use to improve their mental health and well-being.

We don't want you to slog through this book from start to finish in one sitting. We have presented it in such a way that you can immerse yourself in these pages whenever and wherever you can steal a moment for yourself.

We invite you to explore each passage, reflect on yourself, and expand your horizons. How does the passage relate to the people in your life? To your own experiences? How might it shape your feelings and reactions to future challenges? Your reflections and interpretations may uncover deeper meanings as you delve further into the book. You may even find powerful mantras that become part of your life.

Some passages may not feel particularly relevant to your life when you explore them the first time. But when the time comes—and it likely will—you can reach for this book for much-needed perspectives on life from real people who have lived, loved, and lost.

Hopefully, this book will leave you with a sense of hope and inspire you to live your life to the fullest. We want this book to lift you up, especially in times of need, so you can appreciate the priceless gift of life we've been given.

You can find wisdom in every human experience, but resolve and self-satisfaction can only come from within.

So brew yourself a drink, make yourself comfortable in your favourite place, and prepare to be sufficiently galvanized to prioritize your needs above all else.

Please note that we did not compromise the integrity of any quotes or poems by modernizing their language. Thus, the quotes reflect the time period during which they were written.

CHAPTER I

LOOKING INWARD

CHAPTER II

INSPIRATION

CHAPTER III

GREAT MINDS

CHAPTER IV

LOSS AND GRIEF

CHAPTER V

LOVE AND RELATIONSHIPS

CHAPTER VI

HOPE

CHAPTER I
LOOKING INWARD

TWO MONKS AND A WOMAN

A senior and a junior monk were traveling together. At one point, they came to a river with a strong current. As the monks were preparing to cross the river, they saw a very young and beautiful woman also attempting to cross. The young woman asked if they could help her cross to the other side.

The two monks glanced at one another because they had taken vows not to touch a woman.

Then, without a word, the older monk picked up the woman, carried her on his back across the river, placed her gently on the other side, and continued his journey.

The younger monk couldn't believe what had just happened. After rejoining his companion, he was speechless, and an hour passed without a word between them.

Two more hours passed, then three. Finally, the younger monk could not contain himself any longer and blurted out, "As monks, we are not permitted to touch a woman. How could you then carry that woman on your back?"

The older monk looked at him and replied, "Brother, I set her down on the other side of the river. Why are you still carrying her?"

Conventionality is not morality.
Self-righteousness is not religion.
To attack the first is not to assail the last.

- Charlotte Brontë

Reserve your right to think,
for even to think wrongly
is better than not to think at all.

- Hypatia of Alexandria

When the axe entered the forest, the trees
said, "The handle is one of us."

- Turkish proverb

We sit in the mud, my friend, and reach for the stars.

- Ivan Turgenev

There are only two people who can tell you the truth about yourself - an enemy who has lost his temper and a friend who loves you dearly.

- Antisthenes

A man can fail many times, but he isn't a failure until he begins to blame somebody else.

- John Burroughs

You wake up every morning to fight the same demons from the night before that left you so tired.
That my dear, is bravery.

- Unknown

As I leave my childhood home, I want to ask this old house:
"Will you miss me like I miss you?
Will you wonder how I've changed since I left?
Will you keep being my home if I leave my heart behind?"

- Unknown

The monsters were never under my bed.
Because all the monsters were in my head.
I fear no monsters, for no monsters I see.
Because all this time, the monster has been me.

- Nikita Gill

From *Wild Embers and Your Soul is a River* by Nikita Gill © Nikita Gill 2017 and 2018, published by Hachette and Thought Catalog, respectively, reproduced with kind permission by David Higham Associates.

DROWNING

Hypnotized by the rhythmic bobbing of my tapered bough cutting through the lazy morning dew,

My youthful bravado shines, knowing my discarded life jacket is not needed.

I gratify in a well-executed J-stroke as I deftly navigate the winding shoreline,

And unconsciously glance back at the receding eddies brought to life with each pull of the paddle.

I sit silently and gaze into the reflection of the sunrise on the still, glassy surface of the water,

While I endure the buzz of angry mosquitoes and scratch at the vestiges of their feedings,

I'm rewarded with the occasional croaking of a lonely bullfrog,

Or a fleeting glance at a startled deer gracefully bounding into the forest.

I coast a little to take in the pungent, woodsy smell of an overhanging cedar tree,

And eagerly search the passing lily pads, admiring the bravest ones blooming to face the day.

It's taken a lifetime to realize those eddies were taking my anxieties and self-doubt with them,

Dispersing them in the depths of Tamarac Lake, never to be seen again.

Not the intoxicating effervescent fizz weighing down my insecurities,

Only to resurface in a cascade of rising bubbles and be swallowed again.

- Keith Shular

Anger is the punishment we give
ourselves for someone else's mistake.

- Unknown Monk

Critics are men who watch a battle from a high place
and then come down and shoot the survivors.

- Ernest Hemingway

Everybody is a genius. But if you judge a fish by
its ability to climb a tree, it will live its whole life
believing that it is stupid.

- Unknown

Everything has beauty, but not everyone sees it.

- Confucius

I was not myself aware of my own loss, till I sat down to write this history.
I was not, till then, aware of the quiet of my childhood.

- Charles Dickens

One mistake you should never make in this life is to allow yourself to be recruited, by someone, to hate another person who hasn't wronged you. Only a fool inherits other people's enemies as a sign of loyalty.

- Unknown

Once you carry your own water,
you will learn the value of every drop.

- Proverb

Some people die at twenty five
and aren't buried until they are seventy five.

- *Unknown*

To see a world in a grain of sand
and a heaven in a wildflower.
Hold infinity in the palm of your hand
and eternity in an hour.

- *William Blake*

The question is not what you look at, but what you see.

- *Henry David Thoreau*

Living with anxiety is like being followed by a voice. It knows all your insecurities and uses them against you. It gets to the point when it's the loudest voice in the room – the only one you can hear.

- Samantha Gluck

IN HER SOFT EYES

I asked her to marry me in the old sandbox in my backyard, where we jostled as sophomoric kids.

My eyes are fixed on the ceiling of my childhood room, her soft eyes gaze upon me. We lay together, our bodies naked and warm.

"Come back to me," she says, sensing my reticence.
"I never left you," I reply, running my fingers through her silky auburn hair.

This room used to be my prison, my palace of pain and purgatory.

Never knowing when my mother would reload her anger and direct her blind fire from her armchair throne in the living room.

She would follow me through my life like a tongue-slapping Komodo dragon waiting for its prey to give up and die...

But I didn't.

I fell in love with an Irish girl with freckles on her face, a constellation of stars in a clear sky. Wit and grace of words that can pierce metal, or wrap a lonely boy's heart with delectation.

This room is no longer the dungeon of my mind. It has been vivified with love. At that moment I learned that happiness and sadness aren't people, places or things. We carry joy and pain in buckets, spilling over on people around us in unequal measures wherever we go.

I tell my soul mate as I ruminate on the dirty, old, meatless bones of my past, "Never be worried about my silence. It doesn't mean I'm distant. I'm just sitting on a bench with my sorrow, telling him how beautiful life can be as the sun sets on our lives, one day at a time."

- Kevin Mitchell

The pessimist complains about the wind.

The optimist expects it to change.

The leader adjusts the sail.

- William Arthur Ward

Alice: "How long is forever?"
White Rabbit: "Sometimes, just one second."

- Lewis Caroll

No greater desire exists
than a wounded person's need for another wound.

- Georges Bataille

All men make mistakes, but a good man yields when he knows his course is wrong, and repairs the evil. The only crime is pride.

- Sophocles

Detachment is not that you own nothing.
Detachment is that nothing owns you.

- The Bhagavad Gita

Before you embark
on a journey of revenge,
dig two graves.

- Confucius

The bee doesn't waste time trying to convince
the fly that honey tastes better than shit.

- Modern proverb

NOTHING GOLD
CAN STAY

Nature's first green is gold,
Her hardest hue to hold.
Her early leaf's a flower;
But only so an hour.
Then leaf subsides to leaf.
So Eden sank to grief,
So dawn goes down to day.
Nothing gold can stay.

- Robert Frost

He with body waged a fight,
But body won; it walks upright.
Then he struggled with the heart;
Innocence and peace depart.
Then he struggled with the mind;
His proud heart he left behind.
Now his wars on God begin;
At stroke of midnight God shall win.

- William Butler Yeats

CHAPTER II
INSPIRATION

Hopefully, you weren't too hard on yourself in Chapter I. Let's beat the war drum now.

Conquer yourself rather than the world.

- René Descartes

Chapter II should lift you up and inspire you to crush whatever challenges you have in front of you. It will provide the armour you'll likely need to read through Chapters IV, V and VI.

The great soul that sits on the throne of the universe is not, never was, and never will be, in a hurry.

- Josiah Gilbert Holland

If everything around seems dark,
look again, you may be the light.

- Rumi

Be humble, for you are made of earth.
Be noble, for you are made of stars.

- Serbian proverb

I do not regret one moment of my life,
even those that have been difficult or painful.
They have all taught me something.

- Sarah Bernhardt

A healthy man wants a thousand things.
A sick man only wants one.

- Confucius

Showing your emotions to strangers
is like bleeding next to sharks.

- Unknown

Raise your words not your voice.
It is rain that grows flowers, not thunder.

- Rumi

There are two important days in your life.
The day you are born, and the day you find out why.

- Mark Twain

He who has a why to live for can bear almost any how.

- Friedrich Nietzsche

Keep your face to the sunshine
and you cannot see a shadow.

- Helen Keller

Do not follow where the path may lead.
Go instead where there is no path and leave a trail.

- Ralph Waldo Emerson

Never seek revenge. Rotten fruit will fall by itself.

- Mahatma Gandhi

I've had a lot of worries in my life,
most of which never happened.

- Mark Twain

If you are depressed, you are living in the past.
If you are anxious, you are living in the future.
If you are at peace, you are living in the present.

- Laozi

If you want to be happy,
you have to stop living in the past.
Old keys don't unlock new doors.

- Modern proverb

Hurting someone's feelings is as easy as
throwing a rock in the ocean.
But you will never know how deep the rock goes.

- Unknown

THIS LIFE

This, is not how the young boy pretended.

Yet This, is what the young man must contend with.

But This, may one day be an old man's begrudging contentment.

Remember This,
For you get only one chance at Life.

- Keith Shular

Winning isn't everything, but wanting to win is.

- Vince Lombardi

Life is like a piano.
White notes are success.
Black notes are failures.
You need both to play music.

- Unknown

Stupid is the man who always remains the same.

- Voltaire

Strong minds suffer without complaining.
Weak minds complain without suffering.

- Lettie Cowman

Surround yourself with people who fight for you
in rooms you are not in.

- Unknown

Wise men speak because they have something to say;
Fools speak because they have to say something.

- Plato

For what it's worth... it's never too late, or in my case too early, to be whoever you want to be. There's no time limit. Start whenever you want. You can change or stay the same. There are no rules to this thing. We can make the best or the worst of it. I hope you make the best of it. I hope you see things that startle you. I hope you feel things you've never felt before. I hope you meet people who have a different point of view. I hope you live a life you're proud of, and if you're not, I hope you have the courage to start over again.

- F. Scott Fitzgerald

In every walk in nature
one receives far more than he seeks.

- John Muir

Death is the mother of beauty. Only the
perishable can be beautiful, which is why we
are unmoved by artificial flowers.

- Wallace Stevens

It's better to be a warrior in a garden
than a gardener in a war.

- Miyamoto Musashi

Dirty water doesn't stop plants from growing.

- Chinese proverb

If you want to go fast, go alone.
If you want to go far, go together.

- African Proverb

Better an empty house than a bad guest.

- Serbian Proverb

And the gentleness that comes,
not from the absence of violence,
but despite the abundance of it.

- Reproduced with the kind permission of Richard Siken.

Be valuable. Not available.

- Unknown

Behavior is always greater than knowledge,
because in life, there are many situations where
knowledge fails, but behavior can still handle.

- Unknown

Watch your thoughts, they become words.
Watch your words, they become actions.
Watch your actions, they become habits.
Watch your habits, they become your character.
Watch your character, for it becomes your destiny.

- Laozi

Nobody is more inferior
than those who insist on being equal.

- Friedrich Nietzsche

If I have seen further, it is by standing
on the shoulders of giants.

- Sir Isaac Newton

Whoever fights monsters should see to it that in
the process, he does not become a monster.
And if you gaze into an abyss, the abyss will gaze
back into you.

- Friedrich Nietzsche

Do not let birds who can't fly pick at your feathers.

- Anonymous

The birds that were singing in the dew-drenched garden seemed to be telling the flowers about her.

- Oscar Wilde

INVICTUS

Out of the night that covers me,
Black as the pit from pole to pole,
I thank whatever gods may be
For my unconquerable soul.

In the fell clutch of circumstance
I have not winced nor cried aloud.
Under the bludgeonings of chance
My head is bloody, but unbowed.

Beyond this place of wrath and tears
Looms but the Horror of the shade,
And yet the menace of the years
Finds and shall find me unafraid.

It matters not how strait the gate,
How charged with punishments the scroll,
I am the master of my fate,
I am the captain of my soul.

- William Ernest Henley

If you do not change direction,
you may end up where you are heading.

- Laozi

All men have a mind
that cannot bear the suffering of others.

- Mencius

If you are determined to be good,
you must first be determined to be strict with yourself.

- Xunzi

THE ROAD NOT TAKEN

Two roads diverged in a yellow wood,
And sorry I could not travel both
And be one traveler, long I stood
And looked down one as far as I could
To where it bent in the undergrowth;

Then took the other, as just as fair,
And having perhaps the better claim,
Because it was grassy and wanted wear;
Though as for that the passing there
Had worn them really about the same,

And both that morning equally lay
In leaves no step had trodden black.
Oh, I kept the first for another day!
Yet knowing how way leads on to way,
I doubted if I should ever come back.

I shall be telling this with a sigh
Somewhere ages and ages hence:
Two roads diverged in a wood, and I-
I took the one less traveled by,
And that has made all the difference.

- Robert Frost

One does not attain
everything he wishes for.
Winds blow counter
to what the ships desire.

- Al Mutanabbi

I am never stagnant;
I rise from my worst disasters, I turn, I change.

- Virginia Woolf

We can forgive a child who is afraid of the dark;
the real tragedy of life is when men are afraid of the light.

- Plato

YOU ARE THE SUN

The universe did not breathe star fire into your bones just so you could burn yourself out over someone who treats you like a cigarette break.

You deserve someone who knows there is stardust in your veins and that you are the sun.

And the sun does not shine because someone else wants it to. It shines because that is what it was born to do.

- Nikita Gill

From *Wild Embers and Your Soul is a River* by Nikita Gill © Nikita Gill 2017 and 2018, published by Hachette and Thought Catalog, respectively, reproduced with kind permission by David Higham Associates.

IF-

If you can keep your head when all about you

Are losing theirs and blaming it on you,

If you can trust yourself when all men doubt you,

But make allowance for their doubting too; If you can wait and not be tired by waiting, Or being lied about, don't deal in lies, Or being hated, don't give way to hating, And yet don't look too good, nor talk too wise:

If you can dream-and not make dreams your master;

If you can think-and not make thoughts your aim;

If you can meet with Triumph and Disaster And treat those two impostors just the same; If you can bear to hear the truth you've spoken

Twisted by knaves to make a trap for fools,

Or watch the things you gave your life to, broken,

And stoop and build 'em up with worn-out tools:

If you can make one heap of all your winnings

And risk it on one turn of pitch-and-toss,

And lose, and start again at your beginnings

And never breathe a word about your loss; If you can force your heart and nerve and sinew

To serve your turn long after they are gone,

And so hold on when there is nothing in you Except the Will which says to them: 'Hold on!'

If you can talk with crowds and keep your virtue,

Or walk with Kings-nor lose the common touch,

If neither foes nor loving friends can hurt you,

If all men count with you, but none too much;

If you can fill the unforgiving minute With sixty seconds' worth of distance run, Yours is the Earth and everything that's in it, And - which is more - you'll be a Man, my son!

- Rudyard Kipling

Until the lion learns how to write,
every story will glorify the hunter.

- African proverb

Always do sober what you said you'd do drunk.
That will teach you to keep your mouth shut.

- Ernest Hemingway

The only true wisdom is in knowing you know nothing.

- Socrates

Thousands of candles can be lighted from a single candle, and the life of that candle will not be shortened. Happiness never decreases by being shared.

- Buddha

CHAPTER III
GREAT MINDS

MARCUS AURELIUS

Stoic Philosopher and Roman Emperor

We'd like to take a chapter to focus on some of the writings of Marcus Aurelius, a Stoic philosopher and former Roman emperor who ruled from 161 to 180 AD.

His writings and meditations focus on living your best possible life. They are widely known and, remarkably, still in practice today.

We have also included writings in this chapter from other great minds who have contemplated similar themes.

FIVE PERSPECTIVES ON LIFE

ONE

Control your perception. Everything we hear is an opinion, not a fact. Everything we see is a perspective, not the truth.

TWO

Accept what you cannot change. Accept the things to which fate binds you. Love the people with whom fate brings you together, and do so with all your heart.

THREE

Focus on the present moment. Do not dwell
on the past. Do not dream of the future.
Concentrate the mind on the present moment.

FOUR

Practice gratitude. When you arise in the
morning, think of what a precious privilege it is
to be alive, to breathe, to think, to enjoy, and to love.

FIVE

Embrace adversity as an opportunity for growth.
The impediment of action advances action.
What stands in the way becomes the way.

AURELIUS' MEDITATIONS

The best revenge is not to be like your enemy.

The happiness of your life depends on the quality of your thoughts. The nearer a man comes to a strong mind, the closer he is to strength.

I have often wondered how it is that every man loves himself more than all the rest of mankind, but yet sets less value on his own opinion of himself than on the opinion of others.

It's silly to try to escape other people's faults. They are inescapable. Just try to escape your own.

Waste no more time arguing about what a good man should be. Be one.

You shouldn't give circumstances the power
to rouse anger, for they don't care at all.

It's a disgrace in this life when the soul surrenders first
while the body refuses to.

The object of life is not to be on the side of the majority,
but to escape finding oneself in the ranks of the insane.

The art of living is more like wrestling than dancing,
because an artful life requires being prepared to meet
and withstand sudden and unexpected attacks.

The first rule is to keep an untroubled spirit.
The second is to look things in the face and know them
for what they are.

So, other people hurt me? That's their problem. Their character and actions are not mine. What is done to me is ordained by nature; what I do is by my own.

Never let the future disturb you. You will meet it, if you have to, with the same weapons of reason that today arm you against the present.

Blame no one. Set people straight, if you can. If not, just repair the damage. And suppose you can't do that either. Then where does blaming people get you? No pointless actions.

If you are distressed by anything external, the pain is not due to the thing itself, but to your estimate of it; and this you have the power to revoke at any moment.

- Marcus Aurelius

STOICISM

Stoicism is an excellent school of philosophy to consider when focusing on oneself. Often categorized as a religion, it emphasizes courage, temperance, justice, and wisdom. It is, however, important to take its teachings at face value.

Some believe Stoicism can promote a lack of emotion, which, in turn, can lead one to grapple with the so-called passivity problem. If we focus only on our character, reactions, and actions as Stoicism proposes and put no effort into things that lie beyond our direct control, some argue it can cause a Stoic to remain passive on broader issues such as climate change or political issues where the need for a larger conglomerate of people is pivotal to induce change.

A million voices are always better than one. However, if an individual has the clarity of mind to strengthen their mental fortitude through a Stoic mindset, it may have a the ripple effect throughout society, which could translate into a very positive social structure for our future.

Here are some more powerful words from more incredible minds.

Quality is not an act, it is a habit.

- Aristotle

Normality is a paved road.
It's comfortable to walk on,
but no flowers grow.

- Vincent van Gogh

Focus on improving yourself, not proving yourself.

- Unknown

Yesterday I was clever, so I wanted to change the world. Today I'm wise, so I'm changing myself.

- Rumi

Never let your loyalty keep you in situations your common sense should have got you out of.

- Anonymous

A bird on a tree is never afraid of a branch breaking, because his trust isn't in the branch but in his own wings.

- Unknown

We drink the poison our minds pour for us
and wonder why we feel sick.

- Rumi

Resentment is like taking poison
and waiting for the person to die.

- Saint Augustine

We have two ears and one mouth so that we can
listen twice as much as we speak.

- Epictetus

We are more concerned about the
things we should avoid than about the
things we should embrace.

- *Chysippus*

When a flower doesn't bloom you fix the
environment in which it grows, not the flower.

- *Well-known educational proverb*

A man is not old until regrets
take the place of dreams.

- *John Barrymore*

Well-being is attained little by little,
and nevertheless is no little thing.

- *Zeno of Citium*

Indulge us. List all the things you love in life below. When you are finished, turn the page.

_____

_____

_____

_____

_____

How long did it take to list yourself, if you did at all?

Integrity is not something you show others.
It is how you behave behind their back.

- *Unknown*

There's something wrong with your character
if opportunity controls your loyalty.

- *Unknown*

Speak only if it improves upon the silence.

- *Mahatma Gandhi*

Go forward while you can, but if your strength fails you,
sit down near the road and gaze without anger or envy
at those who pass by. They don't have far to go, either.

- *Ivan Turgenev*

Every human being has something to teach others. We each see the world differently, and our perceptions dictate our responses.

Habitually looking for the worst in people and circumstances will weaken your character, as it denies you new opportunities and fresh perspectives. However, it can help identify and protect you from pernicious life choices.

Perceive things as they are without applying preconceived notions and rigid rules, or you will no doubt continue to struggle to find a balance between reluctance and obligatory thinking.

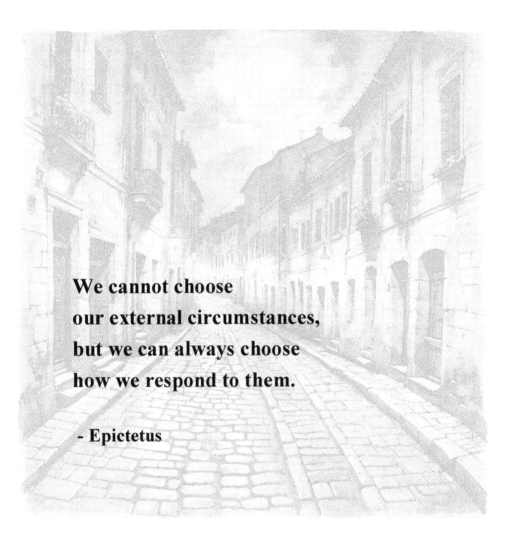

We cannot choose
our external circumstances,
but we can always choose
how we respond to them.

- Epictetus

CHAPTER IV
LOSS AND GRIEF

Unfortunately, we can't begin to talk about love without accepting that what we cherish can be taken away.

Losing people in your life is challenging. Coping with loss can leave us broken and stuck in the past. But it can also help heal the wounds in our souls with the memories and lessons they taught us.

Flowers are beautiful, but they die. Lovers make us feel alive, but sometimes only for a fleeting moment. Eventually, we're left to pick up the pieces.

Chapter IV may be a challenging read, but it has the power to change how you view the world, helping you better cope with major losses in your life.

Unable are the Loved to die
For Love is Immortality,
Nay, it is Deity-

Unable they that love-to die
For Love reforms Vitality
Into Divinity.

- Emily Dickinson

To the dead, nothing is lost;
to the living, nothing is ever found.

- Ralph Waldo Emerson

What we have once enjoyed we can never lose.
All that we deeply love becomes a part of us.

- Helen Keller

The same lesson will appear in different forms
until you learn to respond differently.

- Buddhist proverb

Death, a cause of terror to the sinner,
is a blessed moment for him who has
walked in the right path.

- James Joyce

Though nothing can bring back the hour
Of splendor in the grass, of glory in the flower;
We will grieve not, rather find
Strength in what remains behind;
In the primal sympathy
Which having been must ever be...

-William Woodsworth

I SHALL FORGET YOU PRESENTLY MY DEAR

I shall forget you presently, my dear,
But I'll be back again in a while;
And yet, if I could do it all again,
I would come back and try to be the same.

I shall forget you presently, my dear,
But if you come back again in a while,
And I see you standing there in my dream,
I'll try to forget you again, and smile.

- *Edna St. Vincent Millay*

THE SQUEAKY WHEEL

I heard the squeaky wheel
wobbling down the walkway to my house.
I laid, staring at the ceiling,
sinking deeper into the couch.

His screeching and the rattling metal
pierced a hole right through my soul.
The cacophony was oblivious
to my pounding head and vomit in a bowl.

But someone should have been there for him -
it wasn't all his fault.
Instead of getting greased that morning,
he bore the dead weight of my Mom.

I forgive that squeaky wheel though -
Such a solemn role he played.
Now, I must forgive myself
and unburden my heart of that weight.

- Keith Shular

They that love beyond the world
cannot be separated by it.
Death cannot kill what never dies.

- *William Penn*

True friends are never apart,
maybe in distance but never in heart.

- *Anonymous*

We could never learn to be brave and patient,
if there were only joy in the world.

- *Helen Keller*

To die will be an awfully big adventure.

- J. M. Barrie

The loss of a friend is like that of a limb;
time may heal the anguish of the wound,
but the loss cannot be repaired.

- Robert Southey

Give me that man
That is not passion's slave, and I will wear him
In my heart's core, ay, in my heart of heart,
As I do thee.

- William Shakespeare

War does not determine who is right.

It only determines who is left.

- Unknown

BECAUSE I COULD NOT STOP FOR DEATH

Because I could not stop for Death –
He kindly stopped for me –
The Carriage held but just Ourselves –
And Immortality.

We slowly drove - He knew no haste
And I had put away
My labor and my leisure too,
For His Civility –

We passed the School, where Children strove
At Recess - in the Ring –
We passed the Fields of Gazing Grain –
We passed the Setting Sun –

Or rather - He passed Us –
The Dews drew quivering and chill –
For only Gossamer, my Gown –
My Tippet-only Tulle –

We paused before a House that seemed
A Swelling of the Ground –
The Roof was scarcely visible –
The Cornice - in the Ground –

Since then- 'tis Centuries- and yet
Feels shorter than the Day
I first surmised the Horses' Heads
Were toward Eternity –

- Emily Dickinson

REMEMBER

Remember me when I am gone away,
Gone far away into the silent land;
When you can no more hold me by the hand,
Nor I half-turn to go yet turning stay.

Remember me when no more day by day
You tell me of our future that you planned:
Only remember me; you understand
It will be late to counsel then or pray.

Yet if you should forget me for a while
And afterwards remember, do not grieve:
For if the darkness and corruption leave
A vestige of the thoughts that once I had,
Better by far you should forget and smile
Than that you should remember and be sad.

- Christina Rossetti

I don't distance myself from people
to teach them a lesson.
I distance myself
because I finally learned mine.

- Unknown

The hottest love has the coldest end.

- Socrates

"Why should I not go back to my ex-girlfriend?" I asked
my grandfather. He replied, "If you see the same tree
twice in the forest, it's because you are lost."

- Unknown

A LOVE THAT WOULD NEVER BE

"Mother" is what I had always known her to be.

Darkness and despondency shackled her mind to the point she could not see.

The small, fragile boy who yearned to be loved, no higher than her knee.

For darkness cloaked her tight as she wept to be free.

My mother left, never to return, suffocating the child who still lives - inside of me.

- Kevin Mitchell

Self pity is our worst enemy and if we yield to it, we can never do anything wise in this world.

- Helen Keller

The greatest loss is what dies inside us while we live.

- Norman Cousins

If you want to learn what someone fears losing, watch what they photograph!

- Unknown

Death is the mother of beauty; hence, from the inmost need of their own nature, the poets of all ages have tried to depict it as a symbol of beauty.

- James Joyce

Nowadays people know the price of everything and the value of nothing.

- Oscar Wilde

If you pick up a starving dog and make him prosperous, he will not bite you. This is the difference between dog and man.

- Mark Twain

GRANDFATHER

When my grandfather was a boy
The meadow-flowers bloomed bright and fair;
And I can still remember well
How he would take me there.

He'd say, "You see, my child, my child,
The world is full of wondrous things,
And I must teach you to rejoice
In all the joy that living brings."

His voice was kind and his heart was true,
And in his love I found my own;
So when he died I wept for him
As for a dear one gone.

- *James Whitcomb Riley*

To be yourself in a world that is constantly trying to make you in to something else is the greatest accomplishment.

- Ralph Waldo Emerson

I know you're not here. I may never see your face again, but I feel you with me, tied onto me like a phantom limb.

- Unknown

What a mother sings to the cradle
goes all the way down to the coffin.

- Henry Ward Beecher

I miss you deeply, unfathomably, senselessly, terribly.

- Franz Kafka

The day your soul left this earth, was the day mine did too.
My heart no longer beats the same.
My eyes no longer see the same.
My mind no longer thinks the same.
While I'm physically here, my soul is with yours.
Bound together in the stars.

- Folk wisdom

THE WILLOW TREE

I hold my father's hand as I sit in a hospital chair, hanging off superfluous words that remain unspoken.

I tell my father about the willow tree I saw yesterday at a farmers market. I saw the sun peeking through the tree's whispy leaves, as I sat alone in a Muskoka chair sipping my tea. I took in everything. Time slowed to a crawl, as my friends sifted through trinkets and trash at the stalls. Its leaves rustled like it's whispering something only I should know. I remembered that sharp cool breeze. It shoulder bumps me back to my father's room.

I hold his hand, gently mapping out its wrinkles with my fingers. I let the tears hit the linoleum floor, like butter in a dish melting in the summer sunlight.

I get up, grip his duffel bag of belongings, and tremble. I want to scream, shout, but instead I allow my soul to clench its fists and pound sand... I turn the faucet to my pain off and breathe.

My pain is nothing these walls haven't heard before. Like spitting into an abyss, waiting for it to make a sound. I say goodbye. I kiss his cold forehead and dry his face of my tears one last time.

I feel nothing but also everything, completely and deeply, standing there soaking in my equanimity.

I finally understand the willow tree.

I finally understand what it is to be... lonely.

- Kevin Mitchell

I THANK GOD

I thank God for my life,
For the breath of heaven within me,
For the beauty of the earth and sky,
For the wonder of the sea and the stars.

I thank God for the gift of joy,
For the strength to endure,
For the love that binds me to the world,
And for the faith that guides my way.

I thank God for my friends,
For their kindness and their support,
For their laughter and their tears,
And for the light they bring to my days.

I thank God for every moment,
For each sunrise and sunset,
For the trials that have made me strong,
And for the blessings I have received.

- Helen Keller

REQUIEM

Under the wide and starry sky,
Dig the grave and let me lie.
Glad did I live and gladly die,
And I laid me down with a will.

This be the verse you grave for me:
Here he lies where he longed to be;
Home is the sailor, home from sea,
And the hunter home from the hill.

- Robert Louis Stevenson

CHAPTER V
LOVE AND RELATIONSHIPS

Words have the power to fill your heart and soul with joy.

Whether reflecting on your first kiss or your first meaningful relationship, Chapter V will hopefully rekindle that magic or remind you to appreciate those in your life who give you the greatest joy.

We don't know what the purpose of life is. However, we do believe our ability to give and receive love is the most satisfying human experience.

I'm like a fish in love with a bird, wishing I could fly.

- Folk wisdom

What we have once enjoyed we can never lose.
All that we love deeply becomes a part of us.

- Helen Keller

True love cannot be found where it does not exist,
nor can it be denied where it does.

- Torquato Tasso

TO MY DEAR AND LOVING HUSBAND

If ever two were one, then surely we.

If ever man were loved by wife, then thee.

If ever wife was happy in a man,

Compare with me, ye women, if you can.

I prize thy love more than whole mines of gold,

Or all the riches that the East doth hold.

My love is such that rivers cannot quench,

Nor ought but love from thee give recompense.

Thy love is such I can no way repay;

The heavens reward thee manifold, I pray.

Then while we live, in love let's so persever,

That when we live no more, we may live ever.

- Anne Bradstreet

When you give joy to other people,
you get more joy in return.
You should give a good thought to
the happiness that you can give out.

- Eleanor Roosevelt

Friends are the siblings God never gave us.

- Mencius

The price of anything is the amount
of life you exchange for it.

- Henry David Thoreau

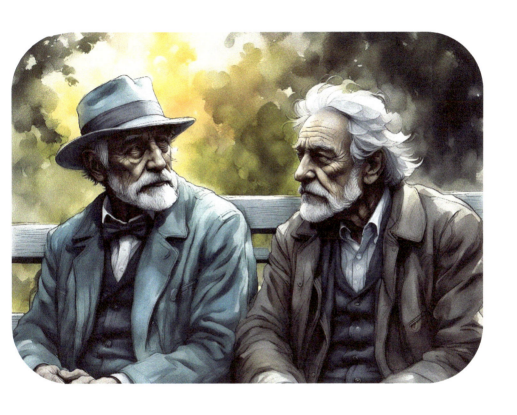

To love and be loved is to feel the Sun from both sides.

- David Viscott

Love is a canvas furnished by nature
and embroidered by imagination.

- Voltaire

Shall I compare thee to a summer's day?
Thou art more lovely and more temperate.
Rough winds do shake the darling buds of May,
And summer's lease hath all too short a date.

- William Shakespeare

I found you without looking and love you without trying.

 - Mark Anthony

Love is the only reality, and it is not a mere sentiment.
It is the ultimate truth that lies at the hearth of creation.

 - Rabindranath Tagore

There's a difference between somebody who wants you
and somebody who would do anything to keep you ...
remember that.

 - Unknown

ON DISHEVELED SHEETS

I laid in her bed on top of disheveled sheets.

She fit in my arm like a perfect puzzle piece.

Smell of coffee filled the air, she yawned.

Kissing her forehead, I try to get up to make her coffee.

She grabs me and pulls me in tight.

"Let it brew," she said.

We make love again, on disheveled sheets.

That was the strongest coffee I've ever had.

- Kevin Mitchell

The best proof of love is trust.

- Joyce Brothers

I know I am but summer to your heart,
and not the full four seasons of the year.

- Edna St. Vincent Millay

True love is eternal, infinite, and always like itself.
It is equal and pure, without violent demonstrations:
it is seen with white hairs and is always young in the
heart.

- Honoré de Balzac

SHE WALKS IN BEAUTY

She walks in beauty, like the night
Of cloudless climes and starry skies;
And all that's best of dark and bright
Meet in her aspect and her eyes;
Thus mellowed to that tender light
Which heaven to gaudy day denies.

One shade the more, one ray the less,
Had half impaired the nameless grace
Which waves in every raven tress,
Or softly lightens o'er her face;
Where thoughts serenely sweet express,
How pure, how dear their dwelling-place.

And on that cheek, and o'er that brow,
So soft, so calm, yet eloquent,
The smiles that win, the tints that glow,
But tell of days in goodness spent,
A mind at peace with all below,
A heart whose love is innocent!

- George Gordon Byron

She was beautiful but not like those girls in the magazines.

She was beautiful for the way she thought

She was beautiful for the spark in her eyes when she talked about something she loved.

She was beautiful for her ability to make other people smile, even if she was sad.

No, she wasn't beautiful for something as temporary as her looks.

She was beautiful deep down to her soul.

She is beautiful.

- F. Scott Fitzgerald

I don't have a favourite place.
I have my favourite people.
Whenever I'm with my favourite people,
it becomes my favourite place.

- *Unknown*

I love you not only for what you are,
but for what I am when I am with you.
I love you not only for what you have made for yourself,
but for what you are making for me.
I love you for the part of me that you bring out.

- Elizabeth Barrett Browning

Forgive me if I stumble and fall for I know not how to love too well. I am clumsy and my words do not form as I wish, so let me kiss you instead and let my lips paint for you all the pictures that my clumsy heart cannot.

- Atticus

If I were to kiss you then go to hell, I would. So then I can brag with the devils I saw heaven without ever entering it.

-William Shakespeare

I caught myself smiling and then I
realized I was thinking of you.

- Unknown

It is good to love many things, for therein lies the true strength and whosoever loves much performs much, and can accomplish much, and what is done in love is well done.

- Vincent van Gogh

If I could give you one thing in life ...
I would give you the ability to see
yourself through my eyes.
Only then would you realize
how special you are to me.

- Unknown

MY CHILD

I cannot name this silence of yours.
Some strange desire is at work in your delicate limbs.
Your shy eyes are hiding a secret they long to tell me.
Your kisses are silently burning through my skin.

Why do you hide your words in your eyes,
And veil them in utter darkness?
Speak but once; I am ready to listen.
Are you the little God that rules my heart?

Ah, the agony of watching your play,
The slow dawning of your youthful passions,
As they stir like young birds,
Flapping their wings,
Impatient to fly into the unknown sky.

I would give my life to watch over you,
To stand by your side as your wings spread,
And to hear the first music of your flight,
As you soar into the infinite freedom of your dreams.

- Rabindranath Tagore

I was never really insane,
except when my heart was touched.

- Edgar Allen Poe

When you're in love with someone, you
aren't interested in anyone else.
If you are, you aren't in love.

- Anonymous

Only those who care about you
can hear you when you're quiet.

- Unknown

I have loved the stars too fondly to be fearful of the night.

- *Sarah Williams*

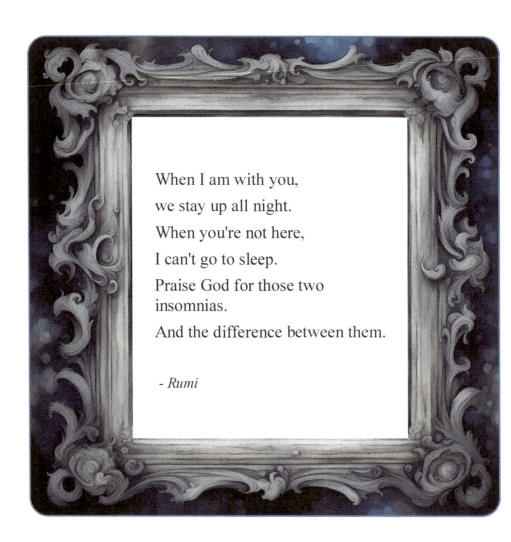

When I am with you,

we stay up all night.

When you're not here,

I can't go to sleep.

Praise God for those two
insomnias.

And the difference between them.

- Rumi

The only way to avoid criticism is to do nothing, say nothing, and be nothing.

- Aristotle

Loneliness can occur even amid companions if one's heart is not open to them.

- Henry David Thoreau

It is easy to love your friend,
but sometimes the hardest lesson to learn
is to love your enemy.

- Sun Tzu

VISION OF THE WORLD

I am a dreamer, I dream of all things,
That keep this world in its place.
I dream of the people, I dream of the things,
That make the world's disgrace.

I dream of the God that comes to a man,
In the darkness of his dream,
And I dream of the man who dreams of the God,
And knows not what it means.

I dream of the lover, I dream of the maid,
That take their pleasure in dreams,
And I dream of the joy that the dreamer knows,
When he wakes and finds it not.

But my dreams are more than dreams to me,
They are the meaning of all things,
They are the revelation of the gods,
And the vision of the kings.

For I have seen the God in the dream,
And I have known the pain of it,
And I have heard the voice of the dream,
And I have felt the strain of it.

And I know that the dream is a vision true,
And that the vision is the key,
To the mystery of the world we live in,
And the dreamer's ecstasy.

- William Butler Yeats

CHAPTER VI

HOPE

Hope is an optimistic state of mind based on the expectation of positive outcomes to the events and circumstances in one's life and the world at large.

In a sense, hope is the unknown. It's that missing puzzle piece you can never fit neatly into your life, no matter how meticulous you are in putting it together. However, if you nurture your body, mind and spirit, you have a much better chance of realizing the end results you ultimately desire.

Hope is the belief that your future will be better than today, and that you're able to make it happen. It involves optimism, motivation and strategy.

Here are some poems and quotes that will ignite your desire and aspirations for the coming days.

To live is the rarest thing in the world.
Most people exist, that is all.

- Oscar Wilde

The only limit to our realization of
tomorrow is our doubts of today.

- Franklin D. Roosevelt

The world breaks everyone and afterward
many are strong at the broken places.

- Ernest Hemingway

DREAM WITHIN A DREAM

Take this kiss upon the brow!
And, in parting from you now,
Thus much let me avow-
You are not wrong, who deem
That my days have been a dream;
Yet if hope has flown away
In a night, or in a day,
In a vision, or in none,
Is it therefore the less gone?
All that we see or seem
Is but a dream within a dream.

I stand amid the roar
Of a surf-tormented shore,
And I hold within my hand
Grains of the golden sand-
How few! yet how they creep
Through my fingers to the deep,
While I weep-while I weep!
O God! Can I not grasp
Them with a tighter clasp?
O God! can I not save
One from the pitiless wave?
Is all that we see or seem
But a dream within a dream?

- Edgar Allen Poe

Sometimes, hope is the last remaining
sinew holding someone together.
Hope is that feeling inside your gut
that says it's not over yet.
Your body, bones and brains might be
telling you it's over,
But hope is what grabs you by the
scruff of your neck
And like a lion, picks up its tired cub on
the Serengeti, and says...
"Die later, get moving."

- Kevin Mitchell

Hope smiles from the threshold of the year to come,
whispering, "It will be happier."

- Alfred Lord Tennyson

The mind that is wise
mourns less for what age takes away;
than what it leaves behind.

- William Wordsworth

For some, hope is like exiting a dark room into the sunlight.
Not only does your path become acutely clear,
but if you turn your inner eye to gaze at what lies behind,
you can see how far you've truly come from the shadows.

- Kevin Mitchell

Chance is always powerful.

Let your hook always be cast;

in the pool where you least expect it,

there will be a fish.

- Ovid

Optimism is the faith that leads to achievement.

Nothing can be done without hope and confidence.

- Helen Keller

**Cease to inquire
what the future has in store;
and take as a gift
whatever the day brings forth.**

- Horace

Hope heals old wounds.

- Unknown

Your mind will take the shape of what you
frequently hold in thought, for human spirit
is colored by such impressions.

- Marcus Aurelius

Hope is important because it can make the
present moment less difficult to bear.
If we believe that tomorrow will be better,
we can bear a hardship today.

- Thich Nhat Hanh

The wound is the place where the light enters you.

- Rumi

I asked my grandmother what I
should do with all this pain;
she said "scrub it clean with love."

- Unknown

The catalyst to hope is not giving up.
Keep pushing forward mentally, physically and spiritually.
If you simply stand still, you run the risk of rotting.

- Kevin Mitchell

Life can only be understood backwards;
but it must be lived forwards.

- Søren Kierkegaard

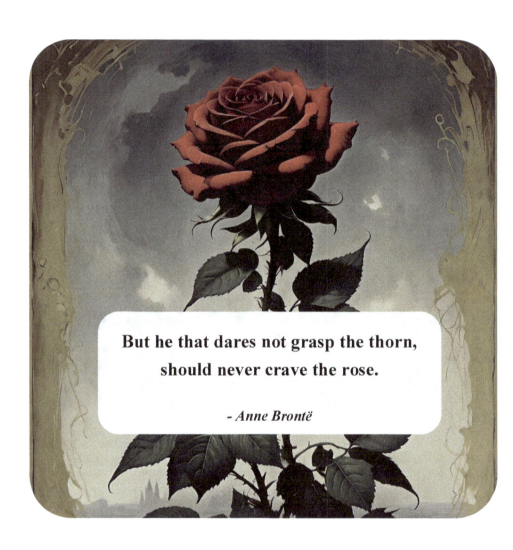

But he that dares not grasp the thorn,
should never crave the rose.

- *Anne Brontë*

Every thing that you love, you will
eventually lose, but in the end, love will
return in a different form.

- *Franz Kafka*

H - hold

O - on

P - pain

E - ends

- Unknown

A setback has often cleared
the way for greater prosperity.
Many things have fallen only to
rise to more exalted heights.

- *Seneca*

In three words, I can sum up everything
I've learned about life:
It goes on.

- *Robert Frost*

HOPE

"Hope" is the thing with feathers –
That perches in the soul-
And sings the tune without the words -
And never stops - at all –

And sweetest - in the Gale –
is heard - And sore must be the storm –
That could abash the little Bird
That kept so many warm –

I've heard it in the chillest land –
And on the strangest Sea –
Yet - never - in Extremity,
It asked a crumb - of me.

- Emily Dickinson

Your skin without your scars
would be like the sky without the stars.

- Nikita Gill

From *Wild Embers and Your Soul is a River* by Nikita Gill © Nikita Gill 2017 and 2018, published by Hachette and Thought Catalog, respectively, reproduced with kind permission by David Higham Associates.

The future belongs to those who
believe in the beauty of their dreams.

- Eleanor Roosevelt

Don't miss out on something that could be great
just because it could also be difficult.

- Unknown

If you want to make an easy job seem hard,
just keep putting off doing it.

- Olin Miller

I suppose I love my scars, because they have stayed
with me longer than most people have.

- Nikita Gill

From *Wild Embers and Your Soul is a River* by Nikita Gill © Nikita Gill 2017 and 2018, published
by Hachette and Thought Catalog, respectively, reproduced with kind permission
by David Higham Associates.

Night is always darker before dawn and life
is the same. The hard times will pass.
Everything will get better and the sun will
shine brighter than ever.

- Ernest Hemingway

FLICKER AND FADE

Over 13 billion years ago, the universe as we know it exploded, flourished and was made.

The light within your soul will soon flicker and fade.

Use that precious time to aid others, foster the illumination they've so delicately laid.

Today is the only relevant reality to think about as we stumble and fall through this life with lumbering doubt.

You may be the only shining clarity for the blind. Be sure you exercise an acute and translucent mind.

The light of all our tomorrows will eventually flicker ... and fade.

The only true treasure we have worth anything is the quality of lives we have made.

- Kevin Mitchell

Hope is the last thing ever lost.

- Italian proverb

If we are to have any hope for the future,
those with lanterns must pass them on to others.

- Plato

Is there another world for this frail dust,
To warm with life and be itself again?
Something about me daily speaks there must,
And why should instinct nourish hopes in vain.

- John Clare

Let your plans be dark and as impenetrable as night, and when you move fall like a thunderbolt.

- Sun Tzu

TO THE FUTURE

Oh, thee, sublime sweet future!

Whose voice is the peace of the world,

Whose presence is the rapture of life,

Whose smile is the dawn of heaven,

Whose breath is the balm of eternal springs.

Shall I not hasten to thee with every beat of my heart,

With every sigh, and with every cry of my spirit?

O radiant, unknown future!

I would speed to thee on the wings of the wind,

To thee who art to crown my life with immortal bliss,

And wrap my soul in the splendor of ineffable light.

- Emma Lazarus

FINAL THOUGHTS

Community, friends, loved ones, books or even a career you enjoy all contribute to the stability of your overall well-being.

Ultimately, the power to fulfill your life with purpose and satisfaction lies within you. It's always been you. It will always be you.

Some say God works through us, and I believe that. But if you don't, then find out what you need to anchor your life and hold you steady when life blows you off course.

Is it your children? Your spouse? A loved one? Or maybe a friend who depends on you?

If you're struggling to find that purpose because your resources are depleted, please reach out for help. Talk to a professional and access resources available to you in your community.

Keith and I found our purposes late in life. We've both had to extend our hands to others reluctantly and with terrifying uncertainty.

Share this book with people you see struggling in life. We don't mean to convince them to buy it. We mean to give it to them.

Our ultimate goal is that this book will ripple outward and touch people who are drowning in fear, anxiety, anger and depression. It's meant to be a life jacket to keep you afloat while you gather the courage to seek help.

Please don't act on a final solution to temporary problems.

Ask for help if you or someone you know is contemplating suicide.

Thank you for reading our book.

Kevin Mitchell & Keith Shular.

LITERARY INDEX

LITERARY INDEX

LITERARY INDEX

ABOUT THE AUTHORS

Kevin Anthony Mitchell

 Kevin was born in Barrie, Ontario, Canada, on March 20th, 1979, to Valerie and Tony Mitchell into a middle-class family.

In 2001, at the age of 21, he chose to live and work in Ireland.

During that time, he traveled to England, Wales, Amsterdam, Italy, Switzerland and the United States of America before returning to Canada in 2007.

Once home, he studied Addictions and Community Services at a community college. He worked for over 15 years with group home children, young adults with autism, and the homeless community.

He currently works with children and is a Christian who regularly supports his community and attends services regularly.

Keith E. J. Shular

 Keith was born on November 18, 1975, in a circular tower known as Scarborough General Hospital in Ontario. Just as his infant self probably struggled to orient himself in a round room, so has Keith struggled to orient himself throughout much of his life.

Rather than admit he still doesn't know what he wants to be when he grows up, he prefers to liken himself to a modern-day. Renaissance man. Some of his interests include solitude and Mother Nature; science and engineering; history and archaeology; music, guitar and sound engineering; sketching, painting and wood carving, as well as starting and not completing projects.

After forging a career as a senior environmental engineer, Keith studied health sciences and pharmacy and has now embraced his passion for helping people living with mental illness and addiction.

This book contains literary works and quotes from some of humanity's greatest philosophers, poets and thinkers.

We have made every effort to credit the original sources when possible. When it was not possible to identify an original source, we credited it as anonymous or unknown.

All artwork was created using digital tools based on concepts and preliminary sketches by the authors.

www.ingramcontent.com/pod-product-compliance
Lightning Source LLC
LaVergne TN
LVHW012330060326
832902LV00011B/1811